Rubáiyát of Omar Khayyám

Rubáiyát of Omar·Khayyám

Rendered into English verse
by Edward Fitzgerald

Introduction and notes by
Reynold Alleyne Nicholson

Illustrations by
René Bull

BRACKEN
BOOKS

500010428

This edition published 1995 by Bracken Books, an imprint of
Studio Editions Ltd, Princess House, 50 Eastcastle Street,
London W1N 7AP, England.

Copyright © this edition 1995 Studio Editions Ltd
Decorative borders by Willy Pogány all rights reserved
Eric Dobby Publishing Ltd

ISBN 1 85891 082 X

Printed and bound in the UK

CONTENTS

LIST OF COLOUR ILLUSTRATIONS

By René Bull

LIST OF COLOUR ILLUSTRATIONS

INTRODUCTION

It is important that European readers who seek information concerning the life and character of Omar Khayyám should realise how little is known definitely, notwithstanding the enormous number of books, commentaries, and articles which have been written on this subject during the last fifty years. A great deal of 'Omarian' literature is deplorably uncritical, and it is only recently that scientific researches, based on the original authorities, have been undertaken. Though mainly negative, the results of modern Oriental scholarship, starting from Schukovski's famous article on *Omar Khayyám and the Wandering Quatrains* (1897), have at least cleared the ground and defined the limits within which a solid construction may be raised. These limits are exceedingly narrow in the present state of our knowledge, and leave no room for such fanciful portraits of the poet as have hitherto been customary. We know next to nothing of his life or the society in which he moved, and the few authentic records do not take us far towards an intimate conception of his character. "But," the reader may object, "we have his poetry: surely the truth, or some clue to it, will be found there." To this the answer is, that while in one sense we have Omar's poetry, in another sense we have not. Many quatrains included in the so-called *Rubáiyát of Omar Khayyám* are unquestionably his. A very large proportion, however – probably not less than nine-tenths – of the whole collection is the work of other hands. Both in style and matter the spurious quatrains are indistinguishable from the genuine. It is impossible, except in one or two isolated instances, to decide from the evidence before us whether Omar wrote any particular *rubái* among the thousands which pass under his name.

For the reasons here briefly stated, Omar's personality must be regarded as an insoluble problem, although its general features, I think, may be guessed at. The trustworthy reports of his life are too scanty to provide even the outlines of an accurate historical sketch, while hardly a ray of light can reach us through the mass of foreign material in which his poetry lies inextricably embedded.

It follows that our attention will be transferred from Omar to the *Rubáiyát* themselves, which are not the product of a single age or of an individual mind, but the many-sided expression of a people's spiritual and intellectual life, the work of many poets, known and unknown, covering a period of six centuries. In this respect the Persian collection resembles the Greek Anthology, but instead of being classified according to subject the contents of the former are arranged in the alphabetical sequence of their rhymes.

What I have to say in this Introduction falls under three heads: firstly, the life and character of Omar; secondly, the

Rubáiyát as they have come down to us; and lastly, FitzGerald's poem, in which he has woven the scattered threads of the Persian original into one complete and imperishable masterpiece.

I
THE LIFE AND CHARACTER OF OMAR KHAYYÁM

Omar Khayyám (or Khayyámí) was born, probably at Níshápúr, in the north-east of Persia, between 1025 and 1050 A.D. His surname, Khayyám (Tent-maker), does not prove that he or his father was actually engaged in that trade, but corresponds to many English names of industrial derivation, *e.g.* Tanner, Mercer, Goldsmith. The familiar story of his friendship at Níshápúr with two schoolfellows who afterwards became celebrated – the great vizier, Nizámu 'l-Mulk, and Hasan Sabbáh, Grand Master of the terrible Assassins – although it has been traced back to a comparatively early date (about 1300 A.D.), is open to criticism on chronological and other grounds, and bears all the marks of being one of those romantic fictions with which Oriental writers are fond of embellishing the lives of illustrious men. That Omar received an excellent education may be taken for granted. We first hear of him in 1074 A.D. as an eminent astronomer presiding over a commission appointed by Sultan Maliksháh to reform the calendar. During the period of political and religious strife which ensued upon the death of Maliksháh, in 1092 A.D., he seems to have left his native town; but we do not know how long his absence lasted, and whether it was voluntary or inspired by fears for his safety. In 1112 A.D. he was at Balkh and uttered the famous prediction, "My grave will be in a spot where the trees will shed their blossoms on me twice a year." Two years later, while staying in the house of the Prime Minister, Sadru'ddín Muhammad, at Merv, he showed his skill in astrology by promising the king fair weather for a hunting expedition. The year of his death is uncertain, but the date usually given, 1123 A.D., has nothing against it, and agrees with the testimony of his friend and admirer, Nizámí 'Arúzí of Samarcand, who, on visiting his grave at Níshápúr, in 1135 A.D., observes that Omar "had veiled his countenance in the dust" some years ago.

So much for the external course of his life. Let us now see what impression he made on his contemporaries.

The oldest notice of Omar occurs in the *Chahár Maqála*, or 'Four Discourses,' by the above-mentioned Nizámí 'Arúzí, a professional poet, who lived "chiefly in Khorásán at royal courts, where he had opportunities of meeting many noteworthy persons," and died in the latter half of the twelfth century of our era. This valuable and highly interesting work, of which Professor Browne published an English translation in the *Journal of the Royal Asiatic Society* (1899), is divided into four sections dealing respectively with the Secretarial Art, the Poetic Art, the Science of Astrology, and the Science of Medicine. It is significant that Omar is ranked among the astrologers, and that no allusion is made to his poetry. The two anecdotes told of him descibe the prognostications which I have already mentioned, and how in each case his words were fulfilled. Nizámí expresses the opinion that Omar had not any great belief in astrological predictions, but shared the incredulity of eminent scientists on this point. He calls Omar 'the Argument of Truth' (*Hujjatu 'l-Haqq*), speaks of him with the affectionate reverence due to a master, and says that he had never seen his like in the world.

This is the only contemporary record of importance that has been preserved, but in the *Firdausu 'l-Tawáríkh*, an historical work composed in the first decade of the fifteenth century, we find a citation from Abu 'l-Hasan al-Baihaqí [1] to the effect that he was present at a meeting (of learned men) in Omar's house in the year 1111 A.D., and was asked by him to explain a difficult Arabic verse.

Fuller information concerning Omar is given by several writers of the thirteenth century. As all these passages, which Schukovski published in the original Arabic or Persian with a Russian translation, have been rendered into English by Dr. Denison Ross, and are well known to students, I shall only refer to them in so far as they seem to throw light on Omar's character.

Najamu'ddín Dáya (died 1256 A.D.), author of a mystical treatise entitled *Mirsádu 'l-Ibád*, reckons him among those

---

1 This person, who has not hitherto been identified, is probably Abu 'l-Hasan 'Ubaidu 'llah ibn Muhammad ibn al-Imám Abí Bakr al-Baihaqí, a traditionalist "of little merit." His death at the age of 74 is chronicled in the *Shadharátu 'l-Dhahab*, a manuscript in my collection, under the year 523 A.H. (1129 A.D.).

unfortunate "philosophers and materialists" who have gone astray from the Truth, and quotes two quatrains as evidence of "his utter shamelessness and corruption." Since this is the earliest reference to Omar's *Rubáiyát*, and one of the very few cases in which we can be fairly confident that we have before us a genuine specimen of his poetry, I append a literal translation of the verses in question (Whinfield, Nos. 508 and 126):

> To the circle wherein is our coming and going
> Neither beginning nor end is visible.
> No one in this world can rightly tell
> Whence is our coming and whither is our going.

> When the Lord moulded His creatures out of diverse
>   elements,
> Why did He subject them to decay?
> If they are well shaped, why does He shatter them?
> And if these forms are ill-shaped, whose fault is it?

The same view of Omar is presented by Ibnu 'l-Qiftí in his 'Chronicle of the Sages' (*Táríkhu 'l-Hukamá*). Omar, he says, was a teacher of Greek science, and had an unrivalled knowledge of astronomy and philosophy. His want of religion, though he tried to conceal it, exposed him to attacks which made him more cautious than ever in uttering his real opinions. He performed the pilgrimage to Mecca, not from piety but from motives of prudence, and when he reached Baghdad on his homeward journey refused to meet the learned scientists of that city who were eager to become acquainted with him. Ibnu 'l-Qiftí quotes the following Arabic verses by Omar, with the remark that his poetry is widely circulated, and reveals an irreligious spirit to those who look below the surface.:

If my soul is content with a livelihood sufficient for my needs, which is gained by the labour of my hands and arms,

I am safe from all changes and accidents, and care not whether Time threatens me or flatters my hopes.

Have not the revolving Heavens determined to reduce all happiness to misfortune?

Therefore, O my soul, abide patiently in thy sleeping-place: its towers will not topple down until its foundations have collapsed.

From the 'Delight of Spirits' (*Nuzhatu 'l-Arwáh*), a volume containing biographies of savants by Shahrazúrí, we learn that Omar belonged to the philosophic school of Avicenna, that he was ill-tempered and parsimonious, that he had an excellent memory but disliked teaching, and that his dying words were: "O God, I have known Thee to the full extent of my power: forgive me, therefore, since my knowledge of Thee is my only means of approaching Thee."

Qazwíní, whose account of Omar in his *Átháru 'l-Bilád* closes the list of thirteenth-century authorities, does not add any essential particulars to what has been said above.

The main result of our inquiry as to the view of Omar's character that prevailed among his contemporaries, and those who lived within a period of 150 years after his death, may be summarised thus: Omar was pre-eminently a man of science. This is emphasized by all the authorities. They describe him as one who drank deep at the well of Greek wisdom, and composed many famous works on astronomy, mathematics, metaphysics, and natural philosophy. If they go on to accuse him of free-thought, the same charge was incurred by every Moslem scientist who failed to bring his speculations into line with the Koran and Traditions of the Prophet. And the accusers, from their own illiberal standpoint, were usually right. Omar, like other intellectual men, must have travelled in search of truth far beyond the punctilious dogmas of Muhammadan divinity. As regards his attitude to mysticism, I think the testimony of Najmu'ddín Dáya is decisive. That writer, who was himself an ardent Súfí, condemns Omar in no measured terms as a philosopher and materialist, that is to say, as a declared enemy of mysticism. We are not bound to ratify his verdict, so far as it brands Omar with materialism – a name often flung at philosophers by devout opponents – but his words are weighty as showing how Omar was judged by Súfís in the thirteenth century. It hardly seems possible that Omar, had he been naturally inclined to the mystic's way of looking at things, would have penned the two quatrains which Najmu'ddín quotes against him. Profound study of the exact sciences rarely predisposes to childlike faith in the Unseen or to enthusiastic self-abandonment. In my opinion, it is more than dubious whether Omar wrote any of the purely mystical quatrains, of which there are a considerable number in the collection, although he was, of course, familiar with mystical phraseology, and may have found it a useful mask for sentiments which he might fear to express openly. "The later Súfís," says Ibnu 'l-Qiftí, "are in accord with some of the *outward meanings* of his poetry, but its *esoteric sense* is a biting criticism of the ecclesiastical law."

Omar was a man of science in the first place, a poet occasionally, a freethinker by necessity, in some moods, perhaps, a mystic, but he played with Súfism rather than believed in it. Thus do I read the salient features of his character, using the only evidence available at present. To discuss his religious and philosophical views in detail would be a work of imagination which, with all deference to those who have written on this topic, I have not the courage to undertake. If it be permissible to hazard any conjecture as to his positive beliefs, I should surmise that he accepted Islam in something of the same spirit and, *mutatis mutandis*, with the same reservations which have enabled many distinguished scientists in the Middle Ages and our own times to accept Christianity.

II
THE RUBÁIYÁT

The texts of the *Rubáiyát* vary considerably in extent, the fullest (Add. 1055 in the Cambridge University Library) containing 801 quatrains. The most ancient manuscript, however, which is preserved in the Bodleian Library, contains only 158 *rubáís*; it is dated 1461 A.D., nearly three and a half centuries after the poet's death. A facsimile of this text has been published by Mr. Heron-Allen (London 1898). The Bibliothèque Nationale possesses a manuscript of 349 quatrains, dated 1528 A.D., while 604 are found in one of the same age belonging to the Public Library of Bankipore. There are also several MSS. of seventeenth and eighteenth centuries.

Until a few years ago every one believed that the quatrains collected under the name of Omar Khayyám were substantially by his hand. This presumption received a rude shock in the year 1897, when Professor Schukovski, in a paper which appeared in Russian and was translated into English by Dr. Denison Ross (*Journal of the Royal Asiatic Society* for 1898, pp. 349-366), showed that 82 quatrains ascribed to Omar occur in the works of other Persian poets. Of this number about half belong to three great poets - Farídu'ddín Attár, Jalálu'ddín Rúmí, and Háfiz; the rest are shared by some forty authors of more or less distinction, e.g. Abú Saíd, Avicenna, Firdausí, Anwarí, Saná'í, and 'Abdalláh Ansárí. Since the publication of Schukovski's article the number of 'wandering quatrains' has risen to 101, a total which would be enormously increased if the entire field of Persian poetry were explored in a systematic manner, and if account were taken of anonymous quatrains, either written as variations on those which already formed part of the collection or added to it for no better reason than that Omar being celebrated as a quatrain-writer, it was natural and convenient to ascribe to him any favourite *rubái* of which the authorship was unknown. Even in the oldest and probably least adulterated MS. the proportion of spurious quatrains already discovered and assigned to their authors is twelve per cent: how many have not been, or can never, be detected? As time passed and the texts grew in size, larger accretions of alloy must have continually gathered round the true Omarian metal, which has come down to us indeed, but so effectually hidden that Omar himself might be puzzled to find it again.

✳ ✳ ✳

We shall now take a general survey of the collection, regarding it as an illustrative commentary, by many hands, on various aspects of Persian life and thought. Its keynote is the deep sense of mortality which runs through Persian poetry of all times like a melancholy and haunting refrain. Life is but a single breath, a bubble on the ocean of Non-existence, a flash of light amidst eternal darkness. All things are for ever flitting away, vanishing into the nothingness whence they momentarily emerged. And the world is full of sorrow, so that Omar or another cries out, echoing the Sophoclean μὴ φῦναι μὲν ἅπαντα νικᾷ λόγον:

OMAR KHAYYÁM

Happy the soul that, having come, soon goes,
But crowned with peace is he that never came!

Over Man – a futile, miserable spectre – broods the shadow of
Fortune at her Wheel, moulding the clay puppets and shattering
them, poisoning their brief pleasure, and denying them any hope
of rest.

How tyrant-like doth Destiny disdain
To stretch a pitying hand to helpless pain,
But when she stumbles on a bleeding heart,
Stabs deeper yet and slays once more the slain!

This is the leading motive, or at least the ground work, of
most of the *Rubáiyát*. As natural corollaries we have either
hedonism or mysticism. Exhortations to empty the cup of pleasure, ere it is dashed from our lips, recur with monotonous
frequency.

Drink! close upon the heels of Life comes Death:
Best pass your time in drunkeness or sleep.

"Nay," replies another,

"I dreamed, and heard the voice of Wisdom sing,
'From sleep Joy's lovely rose will never spring.

Have naught to do with Sleep, the spouse of Death:
Drink! in the tomb there's no awakening.'"

Even the great Persian poets are in some degree the slaves of
convention, and draw liberally on the large stock of commonplace sentiments, comparisons, metaphors, and rhetorical finery
which their predecessors have made fashionable. It needs a
genius, like Háfiz, to triumph over this artificiality and charm a
fresh immortal beauty out of the old themes, although in the
rubái we commonly find a simpler, franker, and more forcible
style than elsewhere. Among the contributors to the
Bacchanalian chapter of our anthology few can be said to have
struck a distinctive and arresting note. Oppressed by the riddle
of Life, they turn in despair to wine as the only means of escape
from themselves, and drown all question of Time and Eternity in
a brimming cup. It is often impossible to decide whether they
mean literal intoxication or mystical 'selflessness,' the same
terms being applied to both.

In a lighter vein, we are given reasons for drinking. Wine is
the sworn foe of religion: you do right to drink its blood; it is
promised in Paradise: why should you abstain from it here?
True, it is unlawful, but you must consider by whom it is drunk,
also how much, and in whose company. Besides, God has eter-
nally known that you would drink: do you wish to prove Him
an ignoramus?

The toper's friends are solemnly enjoined to wash his body in
wine, bury it in the tavern, and let his clay stop the mouth of a

wine-jar or be shaped into a goblet, so that in death as in life he may absorb 'the old familiar juice.' His apotheosis is quaintly imagined in the following stanza:

O pure elixir, essence crystalline!
In thee I'll soak these crazy bones of mine,
That whosoever sees me from afar
Will cry, "Whence comest thou, good Master Wine?"

Love, in the ordinary meaning of the word, is scarcely mentioned apart from wine, and is regarded as a pleasing accessory to the latter. Here the *Rubáiyát* reflect Persian poetry, in which the treatment of love may be either sensual or sentimental, but seldom betrays any profound emotion. Where we hear the language of true passion, we may be pretty sure that it belongs to, or is borrowed from, the mystical adoration of the Divine Beloved which has inspired the most splendid and sublime lyrics in Persian literature.

As I have pointed out, it is unlikely that Omar, the man of science, the sceptic, the agnostic, had any real sympathy with the fervid mysticism in which many of his contemporaries found consolation for the intolerable burdens of this earthly life. We can easily believe that he recoiled from its ecstasies with a certain fastidiousness, and let the keen shafts of his wit play ironically on doctrines and practices that were often abused. In Omar's time mysticism had become, to an alarming extent, a cloak for hypocrisy. The fact is recognised and deplored by Súfí writers of the eleventh and twelfth centuries after Christ. Several quatrains in our collection attack these wolves in sheep's clothing, who preyed upon society while pretending to be religious devotees.

> May the glad noise of revels ring out!
> Perish the sanctimonious and devout!
> Be their patched frocks and azure gaberdines
> Trod in the tavern by a drunken rout!

But a far greater proportion of *rubáis* is concerned with the higher aspects of mysticism, and embodies those characteristic ideas which have dominated Persian poetry during the last nine hundred years. The cardinal doctrine of "Unification,' which means that nothing truly exists except God, is stated in different ways, for example:

> My body's life and strength alone Thou art,
> My heart and soul art Thou, O Soul and Heart!
> Thou art my being: therefore Thou art I;
> And I am Thou, since I in thee depart.

> The Spirit which itself diversely drapes,
> As plant or animal, in myriad shapes,
> Deem not that it can die: the Essence still
> Abides, the visionary Form escapes.

As all phenomena are fleeting shows of the one Reality, so all creeds are pale shadows of the one Religion:

> None of the two and seventy sects with mine
> Agrees, nor any faith but Love Divine.
> Saint, sinner, true believer, infidel,
> All aim at Thee: away with name and sign!

Other quatrains illustrate the well-known Súfí doctrines that Truth is only to be found within, that heaven and hell are subjective, that one must die to 'self' in order to live in God, that the highest knowledge consists in unconsciousness or ecstasy, and so forth. Apart from the wine-quatrains, which can generally be interpreted either in a literal or an allegorical sense, this section of the anthology, though large and important, is rather less extensive than might have been expected in view of the mystical associations of the *rubái* (due, in the first instance, to the famous Súfí of Khorásán, Abú Saíd ibn Abi 'l-Khair) and the preponderance of this element in medieval Persian poetry. Omar's reputation as a freethinker and sceptic appears to have checked the ascription to him of purely theosophical utterances.

It is safe, I think, to say that he pondered much on the enigma of Predestination, and that if we could sift the genuine quatrains from the spurious we should find many dealing with this problem, which exercised the minds of Moslems from the earliest times. The Prophet himself was possessed by the conviction that human actions and beliefs are predestined and immutably fixed in advance. Some passages in the Koran imply that Man has freewill, and is responsible for his actions, but the fatalistic doctrine, from which Mohammed only departed involuntarily, or when it suited him to do so, held its ground and became a chief article of Moslem orthodoxy. The sect called Mutazilites, the Rationalists of Islam, sought to modify the absolute and arbitrary nature of Divine power by asserting Man's liberty to act as he liked, and by vindicating the justice of God, who must do what is best for His creatures. They managed for a short time during the ninth century A.D., to get not only their principles authorised but their special test, the non-eternity of the Koran, enforced by inquisition. This however, was a mere episode. The orthodox party very soon obtained the upper hand, which they never again lost. Asharí, the father of Moslem Scholasticism, admitted that men have a certain power of choice created in them by God, but this power produces no effect on their actions, inasmuch as these also are created by God. Thus, "a man writes with a pen and a piece of paper. God creates in his mind the will to write; at the same moment He gives him the power to write, and brings about the apparent motion of the hand, of the pen and the appearance on the paper. No one of these is the cause of the other. God has brought about by creation and annihilation of atoms the requisite combination to produce these appearances."[1] Such is the theory enunciated by the Cadi al-Báqiláni, a celebrated theologian contemporary with Omar.

1 D. B. Macdonald, *Muslim Theology*, p. 204

Omar Khayyám

In reading the *Rubáiyát* one hears now and then the voice of pious resignation murmuring that it is idle to grieve for misfortune or quarrel with the eternal decrees of Providence, but oftener by far comes the cry of revolt, asking, "Is this fair play?" and answering itself with defiant laughter or frivolous mockery.

When He first moulded into life my clay,
The works that thence proceed in black array
Full well He knew: no sin but He ordained it;
Why burn me, then, on Resurrection Day?

If God wills not to me what I have willed,
I ne'er can hope to see what I have willed;
And if what He hath willed is always right,
Alas! how wrong must be what I have willed!

Of course the *advocatus Dei* puts in his word:

To call the eternal prescience cause of sin
Is the extreme of folly, think the wise.

"That may be," rejoins the sinner, "but suppose that God is not the author of evil and we ourselves are responsible, does not He owe us a good turn after all?

My thirst keeps taverns flourishing, and o'er
A thousand broken vows must answer for;

Yet, if I sin not, who will me forgive?
All mercy lies at my unrighteous door.

You will tell me that punishment is the wages of sin. Well, if God gives back evil for evil, He behaves like the rest of us. That is not *my* opinion, however.

Tho' pearls of worship I ne'er strung for Thee,
Nor cleansed my face of sin's foul stain, I see
Hope Thou mayst yet forgive me all, because
I never counted One as two or three.

This stanza expresses the Murjite doctrine that Man is saved by faith, not by works. Another recalls the Zoroastrian idea that the souls of the pious after death meet their own good thoughts, good words, and good deeds in the form of a beautiful maiden, while an ugly hag represents to the wicked their evil thoughts, evil words, and evil deeds; but here it is said that men will be actually transformed into a corresponding shape:

Since qualities shall all requited be,
And portioned to thy wisdom thy degree,
Strive after good: on the Last Day thou'lt rise
Clad in the form that fits thy quality.

Professor Browne remarks that "it is not uncommon for Súfís to describe a man by the form with which they profess to identify him in the 'World of Similitudes.' Thus I have heard a Súfí say to his antagonist, 'I see you in the World of Similitudes as an old tooth-less fox, desirous of preying upon others, but unable to do so.'"[1]

The mollas, ascetics, and zealots are severely castigated:

> Those prayer-mat worshippers like asses go,
> Bearing the burden of a saintly show.

It is better to be drunk with wine than with spiritual pride. Men waste their time in prayer and fasting, in a mechanical routine of devotion which leaves the heart unmoved:

> They pass away, and none brings back the tale
> Of that mysterious world beyond the pale,
> Whose portal opes to true beseeching tears
> When your glib paternosters naught avail.

Agnosticism finds powerful support in the *Rubáiyát*, as readers of fitzGerald's version are aware, but there is no vestige of atheism or materialism.

> The good and evil in this mortal state,
> The joy and sorrow preordained by fate,
> Impute them not to heaven – blind, feeble heaven –
> With which compared *thou* art a potentate.

1 *A Year amongst the Persians*, p. 141.

INTRODUCTION

Man, is not he Creation's last appeal,
The light of Wisdom's eye? Behold the wheel
Of universal life as 'twere a ring,
But Man the superscription and the seal!

In this brief sketch of the *Rubáiyát* I have indicated the prin-
cipal ideas – especially the religious ideas – to which not Omar
alone, but the national genius of Persia, has given terse and
striking expression. Less striking but equally interesting in their
way are the maxims bearing on morality and social life.
Referring any of my readers who desire information on these
topics to Dr. Christensen's admirable *Recherches sur les Rubāiyāt
de 'Omar Ḫayyām* (Heidelberg, 1905), I will conclude with a
few examples chosen at random:

If a sage gives you gall, take it; but if a fool gives you honey,
spill it on the ground.
Uncongenial company is Hell on earth.
Never drink wine with a low fellow, who is ill-tempered and
has no intelligence or sense of dignity.
In these days it is best to make few friends.
Put up with annoyance and seek no remedy; live cheerfully in
sorrow's company and do not look for a sympathiser.
Drink wine and be a robber, if you like: only do good!
If you make one freeman your slave by kindness, that is better
than to set free a thousand slaves.

Goodness both to friends and enemies is good.

Do you wish people to kiss the sole of your foot? Get fame: all bow down to reputation.

Better not eat than eat of everything; better live alone than associate with everyone.

Though money is not the capital of wise men, the garden of the world is a prison to the penniless.

If a man hath a loaf of bread every two days and a sip of water from a broken jug, why should he be the master of his inferiors or the servant of his equals?

III
FITZGERALD'S VERSION OF THE RUBÁIYÁT

I do not propose to discuss the literary history of FitzGerald's poem – a subject which has been exhaustively treated by Mr. Heron-Allen in the introduction to his edition of the Bodleian MS. – but shall make a few remarks on its relation to the Persian original and on the question how far, and in what sense, it may be called a translation.

The Persian collection, as we have seen, consists of a large number of independent quatrains, arranged in the order of their rhymes and totally unconnected with each other: they are not even the work of one author, or of a single epoch, but extend over half a millennium of time and embody the divergent and contradictory points of view of a hundred different writers. Here, then, is an essential distinction between the Persian and English quatrains attributed to Omar Khayyám. The latter, as FitzGerald says, are "most ingeniously tesselated into a sort of Epicurean eclogue in a Persian garden"; and in spite of the varying moods through which it passes, the poem, as a whole, is in perfect harmony with itself and preserves its artistic unity from the first stanza to the last.

It only remains to inquire whether, in other respects, the English version faithfully reproduces the characteristic form and ideas of the original.

As regards the form, FitzGerald, of course, has not attempted the Sisyphean task of imitating the metres of the Persian *rubái*, but he has given us as near an equivalent as is possible in English – at any rate, in English poetry: a stanza of four iambic lines, of which the third one is generally unrhymed, while the first, second, and fourth rhyme together. If something has been lost, more has been gained. The Persian *rubái*, at its best, expresses a single thought lucidly, concisely, and often epigrammatically: it neither borrows light from what has gone before nor lends any to what comes after: it is like a solitary pearl, *totus teres atque rotundus*. Now, FitzGerald's quatrains, although many of them are outwardly complete in themselves, are not independent units but serve a constructive purpose which has vitally affected their form and character. Even if we found them detached from their setting, we could usually recognise them as parts of an organic whole, and in many cases we should be able to replace them in the proper context. The sense flows on – it seldom overflows – through stanza after stanza, broken here and there by sudden turns and precipitous falls, but never losing its way, and gathering force to the end. Such a poem – "most musical, most melancholy" – far outweighs a collection of isolated quatrains, though every one were of the finest excellence.

FitzGerald based his version upon the *Rubáiyát* which he first read in a copy of the Bodleian MS. made by Professor Cowell, and afterwards in the Calcutta edition. It is easy to identify the quatrains which he rendered wholly or partially into English: this has been done by Mr. Heron-Allen in the notes to his translation of the Bodleian MS., published in 1898. FitzGerald, writing to Cowell, makes some interesting comments on his own methods as a translator. "It is an amusement to me to take what liberties I like with these Persians, who (as I think) are not poets enough to frighten one from such excursions, and who really do want a little art to shape them." And again: "My translation will interest you from its form, and also in many respects in its detail, very unliteral as it is. Many quatrains are mashed together and something lost, I doubt, of Omar's simplicity, which is so much a virtue to him.". . . "I suppose very few people have ever taken such pains in translation as I have, though certainly not to be literal." These criticisms of the poet on himself are borne out by a comparison of the corresponding Persian and English quatrains. Even in those which follow the original most closely, the translation never approaches verbal fidelity: a translation in any strict sense it is not, but rather, to quote Professor C. E. Norton, " a re-representation of the ideas and images of the original in a form not altogether diverse from their own." FitzGerald, in fact, allowed himself a licence which no *translator* could have ventured on: he expanded a line or distich into a whole quatrain; he pieced together one or more stanzas from passages which he remembered to have read in different *Rubáiyát*, or in the works of other Persian poets; he omitted, added, altered, and in every way did just as he pleased. Some of his stanzas faithfully reproduce the *meaning* of single Persian quatrains, and on the whole his version may be described as a very free and supremely poetical "paraphrase of a syllabus" of the *Rubáiyát*, which for him were always Omar's. While it reflects certain characteristic ideas with equal truth and beauty, it is far from being entirely true in spirit to the original – how could it be? Persian is not a difficult language, but to read Persian religious and philosophical poetry with full understanding of the sense intended by the writer, is an achievement of which few professed scholars are capable, since it requires not only mastery of the language but also intimate acquaintance with the general history of Moslem thought, and in particular with theology and mysticism. FitzGerald, luckily, did not trouble himself about such matters; the poetry was what he cared for, and he read it by the light of his own speculations and those of the age in which he lived. This is less obvious in the first than in the later versions of the poem. One small but significant example occurs in the fiftieth stanza of the final edition:

A Hair perhaps divides the False and True;
Yes; and a single Alif were the clue –
Could you but find it – to the Treasure-house,
And peradventure to THE MASTER too.

'Alif,' the first letter of the Arabic alphabet, has the numerical value of 1, and is used by mystics as a symbol of the Divine Unity. It was undoubtedly so used by the author of the original quatrain (Whinfield, No. 109):

My soul said, "I desire the mystic knowledge:
Teach me if it be in thy power."
I said "Alif." She answered, "Say no more;
If one is at home, a single letter is enough."

That is to say, the first step towards knowing God is to know that God is One; only realise His Unity, and you know all. 'Unity,' in the mystical sense, implies that nothing really exists besides God, that He is the One Being, and that everything else is Not-being, which reflects Being and thereby *appears* to exist.

Now, FitzGerald does not mean that. It is plain from the context that he uses the letter Alif – partly because of its resemblance in shape to a hair – as a picturesque illustration of his argument (or fancy) that a single elementary truth, if it were fully comprehended, might give a clue to perfect knowledge of God and the Universe. He means, I take it, exactly what Tennyson meant when he wrote:

INTRODUCTION

Flower in the crannied wall,
I pluck you out of the crannies,
I hold you here, root and all, in my hand,
Little flower – but *if* I could understand
What you are, root and all, and all in all,
I should know what God and man is.

This, it may be said, comes to much the same thing as the other. Very likely; but the point of view has shifted from the twelfth century to the nineteenth. The unique popularity of FitzGerald's poem was and is in large measure due to the fact that it spoke to a past generation, as it speaks to the present, of modern problems, conflicts, doubts and perplexities, in language coloured by the remote and mysterious charm of medieval Persia.

Concerning the Notes I need only say that it has been my chief object to explain the Oriental allusions which occur in the poem, and at the same time to call attention to the sources of FitzGerald's inspiration. I have therefore translated (seeking accuracy rather than elegance) a number of the Persian *Rubáiyát*. These translations, besides enabling the reader to verify what has been said above as to FitzGerald's method of composition, and differences between his work and the original, will also, I think, help to elucidate the precise meaning of some passages where the Persian is more direct and transparent than the English.

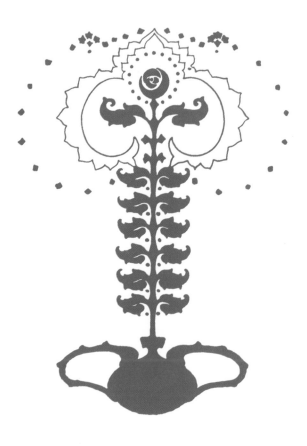

1

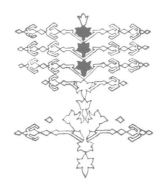

Awake! for Morning in the
Bowl of Night
Has flung the Stone that puts
the Stars to Flight:
And lo! the Hunter of
the East has caught
The Sultán's Turret in a
Noose of Light.

II

reaming when Dawn's Left Hand was in the Sky,
I heard a Voice within the Tavern cry,
"Awake, my Little ones, and fill the Cup
Before Life's Liquor in its Cup be dry."

III

nd as the Cock crew, those
who stood before
The Tavern shouted—"Open
then the Door!
You know how little while
we have to stay,
And once departed, may
return no more."

IV

Now the New Year reviving old Desires,
The thoughtful Soul to Solitude retires,
Where the WHITE HAND OF MOSES on the Bough
Puts out, and Jesus from the Ground suspires.

V

Irám indeed is gone with all
its Rose,
And Jamshýd's Sev'n-ring'd
Cup where no one
knows;
But still the Vine her
ancient Ruby yields,
And still a Garden by the
Water blows.

VI

nd David's Lips are lock't; but in divine

High - piping Péhlevi, with "Wine! Wine! Wine!

Red Wine!"—the Nightingale cries to the Rose

That yellow Cheek of hers t' incarnadine.

VII

ome, fill the Cup, and in the
Fire of Spring
The Winter Garment of
Repentance fling:
The Bird of Time has but
a little way
To fly—and Lo! the Bird is
on the Wing.

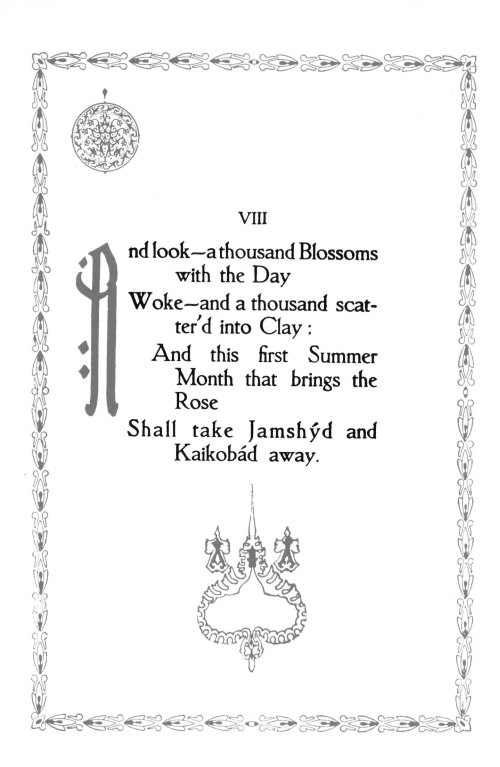

VIII

And look—a thousand Blossoms with the Day
Woke—and a thousand scatter'd into Clay:
    And this first Summer Month that brings the Rose
Shall take Jamshýd and Kaikobád away.

46

IX

ut come with old Khayyám
and leave the Lot
Of Kaikobád and Kaikhosrú
forgot:
Let Rustum lay about him
as he will,
Or Hátim Tai cry Supper —
heed them not.

X

ith me along some Strip of Herbage strown
That just divides the desert from the sown,
    Where name of Slave and Sultán scarce is known,
And pity Sultán Máhmúd on his Throne.

XI

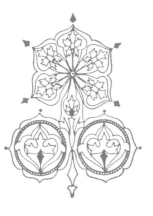

Here with a Loaf of Bread
    beneath the Bough,
A Flask of Wine, a Book of
    Verse—and Thou
    Beside me singing in the
        Wilderness—
And Wilderness is Paradise
    enow.

XII

"How sweet is mortal Sov-
    ranty!"—think some:
Others — "How blest the
    Paradise to come!"
Ah, take the Cash in hand
    and waive the Rest ;
Oh, the brave Music of a
    distant Drum !

XIII

Look to the Rose that blows
about us—" Lo,

Laughing," she says, "into
the World I blow:

At once the silken Tassel
of my Purse

Tear, and its Treasure on the
Garden throw."

53

XIV

The Worldly Hope men set
    their Hearts upon
Turns Ashes—or it prospers;
    and anon,
    Like Snow upon the
      Desert's dusty Face
Lighting a little Hour or
    two—is gone.

XV

And those who husbanded the
    Golden Grain,
And those who flung it to
    the Winds like Rain,
Alike to no such aureate
    Earth are turn'd
As, buried once, Men want
    dug up again.

XVI

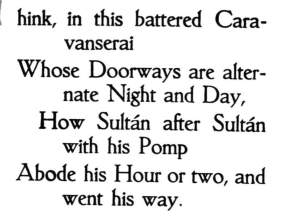

hink, in this battered Caravanserai

Whose Doorways are alter-
nate Night and Day,

How Sultán after Sultán
with his Pomp

Abode his Hour or two, and
went his way.

XVII

They say the Lion and the
Lizard keep
The Courts where Jamshýd
gloried and drank deep:
And Bahrám, that great
Hunter—the Wild Ass
Stamps o'er his Head, and he
lies fast asleep.

XVIII

I sometimes think that never
blows so red
The Rose as where some
buried Cæsar bled
That every Hyacinth the
Garden wears
Dropt in its Lap from some
once lovely Head.

XIX

nd this delightful Herb whose
    tender Green
Fledges the River's Lip on
    which we lean—
  Ah, lean upon it lightly! for who knows
    for who knows
From what once Lovely Lip
    it springs unseen!

XX

Ah, my Belovéd, fill the cup
    that clears
To-day of past Regrets and
    future Fears—
To-morrow?—Why, To-
    morrow I may be
Myself with Yesterday's
    Sev'n Thousand Years.

XXI

o ! some we loved, the love-
liest and the best
That Time and Fate of all
their Vintage prest,
Have drunk their Cup a
Round or two before,
And one by one crept silently
to Rest.

63

XXII

And we, that now make merry
in the Room
They left, and Summer dresses
in new Bloom,
Ourselves must we beneath
the Couch of Earth
Descend, ourselves to make
a Couch—for whom?

XXIII

A h, make the most of what we
  yet may spend,
Before we too into the Dust
  descend;
  Dust into Dust, and under
  Dust, to lie,
Sans Wine, sans Song, sans
  Singer, and—sans End!

XXIV

like for those who for TO-DAY
    prepare,
And those that after a TO-
    MORROW stare,
A Muezzín from the Tower
    of Darkness cries,
"Fools! your Reward is
    neither Here nor There!"

XXV

Why, all the Saints and Sages who discuss'd
Of the Two Worlds so learnedly, are thrust
    Like foolish Prophets forth; their Words to Scorn
Are scatter'd, and their Mouths are stopt with Dust.

XXVI

Oh, come with old Khayyám,
and leave the Wise

To talk; one thing is certain,
that Life flies;

One thing is certain, and
the Rest is Lies;

The Flower that once has
blown for ever dies.

XXVII

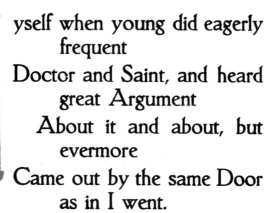

yself when young did eagerly
frequent
Doctor and Saint, and heard
great Argument
About it and about, but
evermore
Came out by the same Door
as in I went.

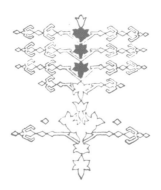

XXVIII

ith them the Seed of Wisdom
did I sow,
And with my own hand
labour'd it to grow:
And this was all the
Harvest that I reap'd—
"I came like Water, and like
Wind I go."

XXIX

Into this Universe, and *why*
    not knowing,
Nor *whence*, like Water
    willy-nilly flowing!
And out of it, as Wind
    along the Waste,
I know not *whither*, willy-
    nilly blowing.

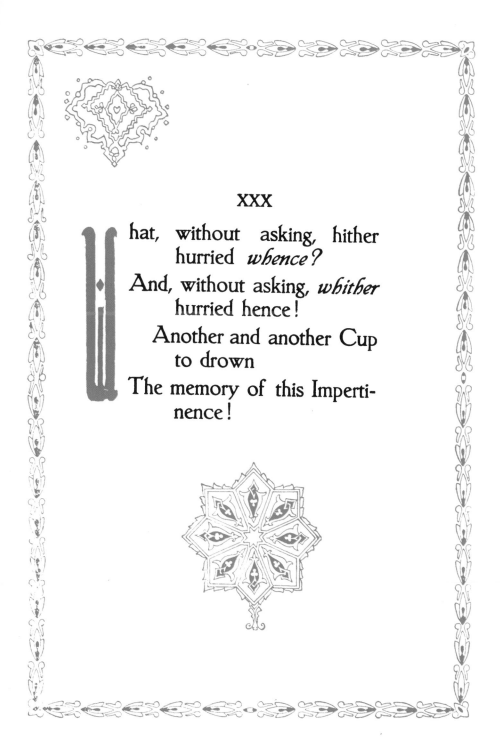

XXX

What, without asking, hither
hurried *whence?*
And, without asking, *whither*
hurried hence!
Another and another Cup
to drown
The memory of this Imperti-
nence!

XXXI

Up from Earth's Centre through
    the Seventh Gate
I rose, and on the Throne of
    Saturn sate,
    And many Knots unravel'd
    by the Road;
But not the Knot of Human
    Death and Fate.

XXXII

here was a Door to which I
found no Key:
There was a Veil past which
I could not see:
Some little Talk awhile of
ME and THEE
There seemed—and then no
more of THEE and ME.

XXXIII

Then to the rolling Heav'n itself I cried,

Asking, "What Lamp had Destiny to guide

Her little Children stumbling in the Dark?"

And—"A blind understanding!" Heaven replied.

XXXIV

Then to the earthen Bowl did
    I adjourn
My Lip the secret Well of
    Life to learn:
    And Lip to Lip it murmur'd
    —"While you live
Drink!—for once dead you
    never shall return."

XXXV

I think the Vessel, that with fugitive
Articulation answer'd, once did live,
    And merry-make; and the cold Lip I kiss'd
How many Kisses might it take—and give!

XXXVI

or in the Market-place, one
    Dusk of day,
I watch'd the Potter thumping
    his wet Clay:
And with its all obliterated
    Tongue
It murmur'd — "Gently,
    Brother, gently, pray!"

XXXVII

A h, fill the Cup:—what boots
it to repeat

How time is slipping under-
neath our Feet:

Unborn TO-MORROW and
dead YESTERDAY,

Why fret about them if
TO-DAY be sweet!

XXXVIII

ne Moment in Annihilation's
    Waste,

One Moment, of the Well
    of Life to taste—

The Stars are setting and
    the Caravan

Starts for the Dawn of
    Nothing — Oh, make
    haste !

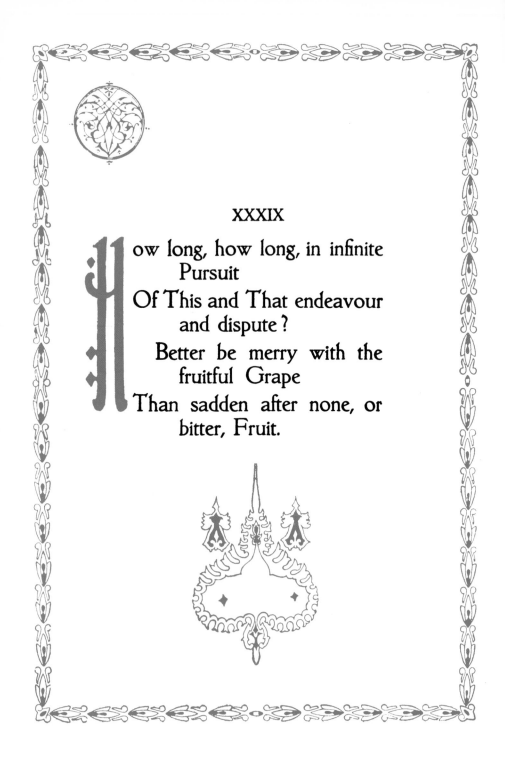

XXXIX

How long, how long, in infinite
    Pursuit
Of This and That endeavour
    and dispute?
    Better be merry with the
      fruitful Grape
Than sadden after none, or
    bitter, Fruit.

XL

You know, my Friends, how
    long since in my House
For a new Marriage I did
    make Carouse:
Divorced old barren
    Reason from my Bed,
And took the Daughter of
    the Vine to Spouse.

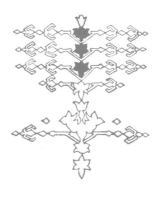

XLI

or "Is" and "Is-not" though
with Rule and Line,

And "Up-and-down" *with-
out,* I could define,

I yet in all I only cared to
know,

Was never deep in **anything**
but—Wine.

89

XLII

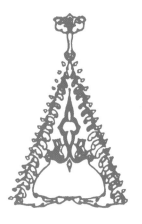nd lately, by the Tavern
Door agape,

Came stealing through the
Dusk an Angel Shape

Bearing a Vessel on his
Shoulder ; and

He bid me taste of it ; and
'twas—the Grape!

XLIII

The Grape that can with Logic
absolute
The Two-and-Seventy jarring
Sects confute:
The subtle Alchemist that
in a Trice
Life's leaden Metal into Gold
transmute.

XLIV

The mighty Mahmúd, the victorious Lord

That all the misbelieving and black Horde

Of Fears and Sorrows that infest the Soul

Scatters and slays with his enchanted Sword.

XLV

ut leave the Wise to wrangle,
and with me
The Quarrel of the Universe
let be :
And, in some corner of the
Hubbub coucht,
Make Game of that which
makes as much of Thee.

XLVI

For in and out, above, about,
    below,
'Tis nothing but a Magic
    Shadow-show,
  Play'd in a Box whose
    Candle is the Sun,
Round which we Phantom
    Figures come and go.

XLVII

And if the Wine you drink, the
Lip you press,
End in the Nothing all Things
end in—Yes—
Then fancy while Thou
art, Thou art but what
Thou shalt be — Nothing —
Thou shalt not be less.

XLVIII

hile the Rose blows along the
River Brink,

With old Khayyám the Ruby
Vintage drink:

And when the Angel with
his darker Draught

Draws up to Thee—take that,
and do not shrink.

XLIX

'T is all a Chequer-board of
    Nights and Days
Where Destiny with Men
    for Pieces plays:
    Hither and thither moves,
        and mates, and slays,
And one by one back in the
    Closet lays.

101

L

The Ball no Question makes
  of Ayes and Noes,
But Right or Left as strikes
  the Player goes;
  And He that toss'd Thee
  down into the Field,
He knows about it all—He
  knows—HE knows!

LI

The Moving Finger writes: and, having writ,
Moves on: nor all thy Piety nor Wit
Shall lure it back to cancel half a Line,
Nor all thy Tears wash out a Word of it.

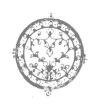

LII

And that inverted Bowl we call
The Sky,
Whereunder crawling coop't
we live and die,
Lift not thy hands to *It* for
help—for It
Rolls impotently on as Thou
or I.

LIII

ith Earth's first Clay They
did the last Man's knead,
And then of the Last
Harvest sow'd the Seed:
Yea, the first Morning of
Creation wrote
What the Last Dawn of
Reckoning shall read.

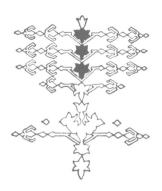

LIV

I tell Thee this—When, starting
from the Goal,
Over the shoulders of the
flaming Foal
    Of Heav'n Parwin and
Mushtara they flung,
In my predestin'd Plot of
Dust and Soul

LV

The Vine had struck a Fibre; which about
    If clings my Being—let the Súfi flout;
      Of my Base Metal may be filed a Key,
That shall unlock the Door he howls without.

LVI

And this I know: whether the
one True Light,
Kindle to Love, or Wrath
consume me quite,
One Glimpse of It within
the Tavern caught
Better than in the Temple
lost outright.

LVII

Oh Thou, who didst with
    Pitfall and with Gin
Beset the Road I was to
    wander in,
    Thou wilt not with Pre-
    destination round
Enmesh me, and impute **my**
    Fall to Sin?

LVIII

Oh Thou, who Man of baser
Earth didst make
And who with Eden didst
devise the Snake ;
For all the Sin wherewith
the Face of man
Is blacken'd, Man's Forgive-
ness give—and take !

LIX

Listen again. One Evening
at the Close
Of Ramazán, ere the better
Moon arose,
In that old Potter's Shop
I stood alone
With the clay Population
round in Rows.

LX

nd, strange to tell, among that
Earthen Lot
Some could articulate, while
others not :
And suddenly one more
impatient cried—
"Who *is* the Potter, pray, and
who the Pot?"

LXI

hen said another—"Surely not
in vain
"My substance from the common Earth was ta'en;
That He who subtly
wrought me into Shape
Should stamp me back to
common Earth again."

LXII

Another said—"Why, ne'er a
    peevish Boy
Would break the Bowl from
    which he drank in Joy ;
Shall He that *made* the
    Vessel in pure Love
And Fancy, in an after Rage
    destroy!"

117

LXIII

None answered this; but after
    Silence spake
A Vessel of a more ungainly
    Make:
"They sneer at me for
    leaning all awry;
What! did the Hand then of
    the Potter shake?"

LXIV

aid one—"Folks of a surly
    Tapster tell,
And daub his visage with the
    Smoke of Hell;
    They talk of some strict
    Testing of us—Pish!
He's a Good Fellow and
    'twill all be well."

LXV

hen said another with a long-
drawn Sigh,
"My Clay with long Oblivion
is gone dry :
But, fill me with the old
familiar Juice,
Methinks I might recover by-
and-bye!"

LXVI

o while the Vessels one by
one were speaking,
One spied the little Crescent
all were seeking:
And then they jogged each
other, "Brother! Brother!
Hark to the Porter's Shoulder-
knot a-creaking!"

LXVII

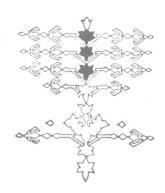

h, with the Grape my fading
Life provide,
And wash my Body whence
the Life has died,
And in a Winding-sheet
of Vine-leaf wrapt,
So bury me by some sweet
Garden side.

LXVIII

hat ev'n my buried Ashes
    such a Snare
Of Perfume shall fling up into
    the Air,
    As not a True Believer
    passing by
But shall be overtaken un-
    aware.

LXIX

ndeed the Idols I have loved
    so long
Have done my Credit in
    Men's Eye much Wrong,
Have drowned my Honour
    in a shallow Cup,
And sold my Reputation for
    a Song.

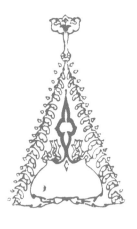

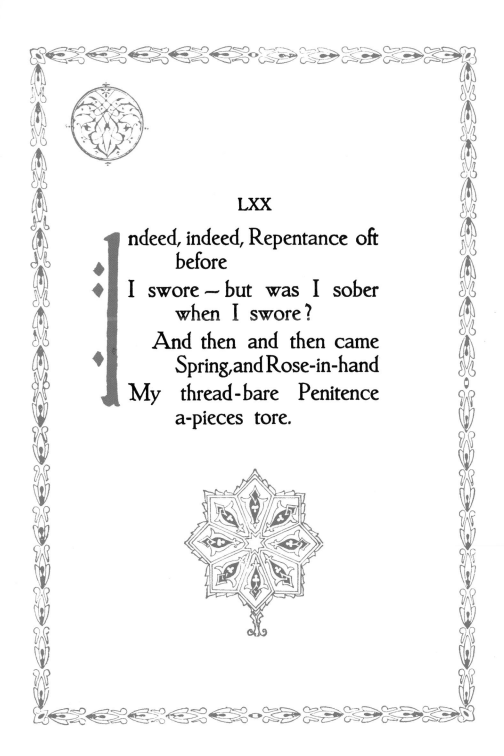

LXX

Indeed, indeed, Repentance oft
 before
I swore — but was I sober
 when I swore?
And then and then came
 Spring, and Rose-in-hand
My thread-bare Penitence
 a-pieces tore.

LXXI

And much as Wine has played
the Infidel,
And robb'd me of my Robe
of Honour—well,
  I often wonder what the
  Vintners buy
One half so precious as the
Goods they sell.

LXXII

las, that Spring should vanish
 with the Rose!
That Youth's sweet-scented
 Manuscript should close!
The Nightingale that in the
 Branches sang,
Ah, whence, and whither flown
 again, who knows?

LXXIII

Ah, Love! could thou and I
    with Fate conspire
To grasp this sorry Scheme
    of Things entire,
    Would not we shatter it
    to bits and then
Re-mould it nearer to the
    Heart's Desire!

LXXIV

h, Moon of my Delight who
know'st no Wane,
The Moon of Heaven is
rising once again:
How oft hereafter rising
shall she look
Through this same Garden
after me—in vain!

LXXV

nd when Thyself with shining
    Foot shall pass
Among the Guests Star-
    scattered on the Grass
And in thy joyous Errand
    reach the Spot
Where I made one — turn
    down an empty Glass!

TAMÁM SHUD

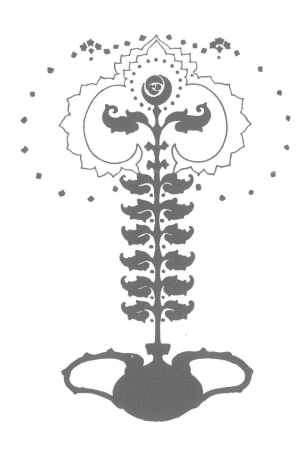

NOTES

I

Among some nomadic tribes the signal for striking camp was given by casting a stone into a bowl. Cf. W. 233:[1]
"The Sun has thrown the noose of Dawn upon the roof,
The monarch of Day has thrown wine into the cup (filled the cup-like sky with ruddy light)."

II

'Dawn's Left Hand' is the shaft or column of light formed by the beams of the sun before it has risen above the horizon. The hour of twilight preceding sunrise is called 'False Morning,' or 'Wolf's Tail' (cf. Greek λυκόφως), alluding, as the lexicologists say, to its length and greyness.

IV

The Persian New Year begins at the vernal equinox, about the 21st of March. It marks the advent of Spring and is celebrated by a joyous festival.

"The White Hand of Moses" refers to a verse of the Koran (vii. 105, xxvi. 32): "*And he drew forth his hand, and lo! it appeared white too those who looked.*" Cf. Exodus iv. 6. In Persian poetry 'hand' (dast or kaf) often means 'leaf.'

"And Jesus from the Ground suspires," *i.e.* the plants shoot up, as though miraculously revived by the life-giving breath of Jesus, whom Moslems call 'the Spirit of God' (Rúhu'lláh).

V

'Irám,' with the epithet 'many-columned,' is mentioned in the Koran (lxxxix. 6) in connection with the prehistoric people of 'Ád, whom God destroyed for their sins, and is variously explained by the Arabic commentators. The Prophet may have had in his mind the ruined colonnades and desolate grandeur of some Syrian town. According to one story, Irám was built on the site afterwards occupied by Damascus, but most authors place it in the desert of Aden, where is still stands invisible though God now and then reveals a glimpse of it to the passing traveller. The poets imagine it as a magnificent Garden-city, an earthly Paradise adorned with superb pavilions and palaces.

Jamshýd, called in the Avesta "the fair Yima of goodly flocks," was a Persian king of the legendary Píshdádí dynasty. The Persians believe that he founded Persepolis, which they accordingly name 'The Throne of Jamshýd.' He is said to have possessed a wonderful cup, round the interior of which were engraved seven lines or rings. Each of these rings depicted one of the seven divisions of the globe: hence the poets often speak of 'Jamshýd's world-displaying cup.'

VI

Following the example of the Prophet, who on hearing the Koran sweetly recited in his presence declared that the reader had 'the voice of David,' Moslems regard the Psalmist as the type of a melodious singer.

The term 'Péhlevi' is generally applied in Europe to the Persian script and literature of the Sásánian

1 W. = E. H. Whinfield, *The Quatrains of Omar Khayyám*, 2nd ed., 1901.

134

period (226-652 A.D.), but the Persians themselves usually mean by it nothing more than some archaic or dialectical variety of their own spoken language; and it has this signification here.

In Persian poetry the Nightingale (*Bulbul*) is constantly represented as the lover of the Rose (*Gul*), a charming fancy, and one that is supported by rhyme, if not by reason.

VIII

Kaikobád was a Persian king belonging to the mythical Kayání dynasty.

IX

Kaikhosrú (Kai Khusrau), wrongly identified by Sir William Jones with Cyrus, was another monarch of the same dynasty as Kaikobád. Firdausí has celebrated the exploits of all these legendary kings in his *Sháhnáma*, but the true hero of that great epic is Rustam, the son of Zál. Zál is said to have been born with white hair, exposed and brought up by a prodigious bird called Símurgh. Rustam, his son by Rúdhába, was a warrior of gigantic strength, who often led the Persians to battle against the Túranian Afrásiyáb and (though at times, like Achilles, he sulked in his tent) never failed to come to the rescue when all seemed lost.

The name of Hátim, a chieftain of the tribe of Tai in pre-Islamic days, has become proverbial throughout the Muhammadan world for hospitality, a virtue most highly prized by the Bedouins among whom he lived. Innumerable stories are told of his extravagant generosity – how he gave away a whole herd of camels for a few lines of eulogy, slaughtered his favourite horse to feast a stranger who asked a night's lodging, and so on. He was a poet too. I venture to quote from my *Literary History of the Arabs*, p. 87, the following verses which he addressed to his wife:

"O daughter of Abdulláh and Málik and him who wore
The two robes of Yemen stuff – the hero that rode the roan,
When thou hast prepared the meal, entreat to partake thereof
A guest – I am not the man to eat, like a churl, alone – :
Some traveller thro' the night or house-neighbour; for in sooth
I fear the reproachful talk of men after I am gone.
The guest's slave am I, 'tis true, as long as he bides with me,
Although in my nature else not trait of the slave is shown."

X

Sultan Mahmúd of Ghazna in Afganistan (998-1030 A.D.) founded a mighty empire including Khorasan, Transoxania, Cashmere, and a large part of North-western India. The line,

"Where name of Slave and Sultan scarce is known,"

suggests the observation that Mahmúd himself was of servile descent, his father, Subuktigín, having been a Turkish slave who rose to eminence in the employ of Alptigín, also a slave originally. "Mahmúd," says Professor Browne, "has often been described as a great patron of letters, but he was in fact rather a great kidnapper of literary men." While he desired the prestige reflected on him by the brilliant array of poets and savants who thronged his court, his shabby treatment of Firdausí is sufficient proof that he did not love culture and learning for their own sakes.

OMAR KHAYYÁM

XI

It is commonplace in Persian literature that nothing can compare with a life of Arcadian simplicity and frugal pleasure, remote from the business of the world.

XII

In the original (W. 108) the last line of this stanza runs:

"For it is pleasant to hear the sound of a drum from afar,"

i.e. "don't let this idle talk of Paradise be dinned into my ears *now*!" 'Drum' implies that the bliss promised to good Moslems after their death is a mere fiction, an empty sound that means nothing.

XIII

FitzGerald took the idea for these verses from the last line of a Persian quatrain (W. 122) which expresses the sentiment that life cannot be enjoyed without money:

"Because the violet is empty-handed, it droops its head,
But the mouth of the rose is laughing because its purse is full of gold."

The golden stamens of the rose are its 'Treasure.'

XIV

W. 243:
"O soul, get thyself all the riches of the world,
And deck the garden of thy pleasure with greenery,
But know that Life is like dew, that settles for a night
On the green leaves and in the morning is gone."

XV

W. 175:
"O heedless fool, thou art not gold that thou shouldst be
laid in the earth and taken out again."

XVI

'Attár relates in the *Memoirs of the Saints* that one day Ibráhím ibn Adham, Prince of Baikh, was seated on his throne, giving audience to his subjects and surrounded by courtiers and pages in due ceremony. Suddenly a man entered, whose appearance struck the attendants with such awe that their tongues sank into their throats, and not one of them dared to ask his name. He advanced and stood in front of the throne. "What do you want?" said Ibráhím. He replied, "I have come to lodge in this caravanserai." "This is not a caravanserai," said Ibráhím, "but my palace: you must be mad." "Who was the owner of this palace before you?" asked the stranger. "My father." "And before that?" "My father's father." "And before that?" "Such and such a one." "And before that?" "The father of such and such a one." "Where are they all gone?" "They are dead." "Then," cried the unknown, "is not this a caravanserai, where one comes and another goes?" With these words he departed and was seen no more.

NOTES

XVII

Bahrám V., generally called Bahrám Gór (Bahrám the Wild Ass) on account of his fondness for hunting that animal, was a famous Persian King of the Sásánian dynasty, who reigned from 420 to 438 A.D. In the 'Seven Pictures,' a romance by the poet Nizámí, it is related that he fell in love with seven princesses whose portraits he found in a secret chamber in his palace of Khawarnaq, and built pavilions of different colours for each of them. He delighted in music and had Gipsies sent to him from India for this purpose. The original lines translated by FitzGerald contain a play on the words *gór* (wild ass) and *gór* (grave).

W. 72:
    "Bahrám who used to catch the wild ass with his lasso -
    Dost thou mark how the grave has caught Bahrám?"

XVIII

W. 104:
    "Wherever roses and tulips bloom,
    They spring from the red blood of a mighty king.
    Every violet that grows from the earth
    Was once a mole on the cheek of a beauty."

XIX

W. 62:
    "Wherever grass has grown on the edge of a stream,
    Thou wouldst say that it has grown from the lip of some angelic creature.
    Beware lest thou set thy foot on the grass scornfully!
    For it has grown in the dust of a girl with tulip cheeks."

XX

W. 312:
    "Come, O my friend, let us not think of to-morrow,
    But make the most of Life that is only a single breath!
    To-morrow, when we journey on from this ancient wine-house,
    We shall march along the road with those who are seven thousand years old."

The 7000 years are reckoned from the creation of Adam.

XXIII

The epigrammatic climax of this stanza is due to FitzGerald.

XXIV

In the original Persian this quatrain (W. 376) is not definitely agnostic, but rather sets forth the view that neither theology nor philosophy can reveal the Truth, which is found by those who have traversed the Mystic Way.

    "Some are pondering on doctrine and religion,

Others are bewildered over doubt and certainty.
Suddenly a crier rises up from his hiding-place,
Saying, 'O ye ignorant! The right way is neither that nor this.'"

The image of the muezzin chanting the call to prayer from the minaret of a mosque is not in the Persian, which only suggests a voice from the Unseen. Lane says (*The Modern Egyptians*, ch. 3): "Most of the muëddins of Cairo have harmonious and yet sonorous voices, which they strain to the utmost pitch: yet there is a simple and solemn melody in their chants which is very striking, particularly in the stillness of the night."

XXV

W. 209:
"Those who encompassed all learning and culture
And, by amassing erudition, became as lamps to their disciples,
Never made their way out of this dark night,
But told a story and went to sleep."

XXVII

This and the following stanza are a 'contamination' of two Persian quatrains.

W. 264:
"I was a falcon who flew hither from the Unseen World,
That perchance from this low place I might soar aloft;
But finding here none learned in the mystery,
I went out by the same door where I came in."

W. 353:
"For a while, in our youth, we went to a master;
For a while we took pleasure in being masters ourselves.
Hear now what is the end of the whole affair:
'We come from earth and we go on the wings of the wind.'"

XXX

FitzGerald has given a turn of his own to the last two lines. The Persian runs (W. 110):

"Since my coming was not by my own will on the First Day,
And my going, with desire unaccomplished, is a fixed resolve (of Providence),
Rise and gird thy loins, O nimble Cup-bearer!
For I will wash down the sorrows of the world in wine."

XXXI

The original of this stanza (W. 303) is ascribed to Avicenna. According to the Ptolemaic system, "around the central, stationary earth revolves a series of nine hollow concentric shells called Spheres or Heavens, arranged one within the other, 'like the coats of an onion.' To each of the seven innermost of these is fastened one of the Seven Planets, which are thus carried round by the spheres in their revolution. These seven planetary spheres are in order, starting from the innermost: (1) that of the Moon,

NOTES

(2) that of Mercury, (3) that of Venus, (4) that of the Sun, (5) that of Mars, (6) that of Jupiter, (7) that of Saturn" (Gibb, *A History of Ottoman Poetry*, vol. i. p. 43). "The Seventh Gate," therefore, means the gate of the Seventh Heaven, over which Saturn presides.

XXXII

The concluding lines refer to the pantheistic doctrine of the Súfís that there is no real existence apart from the One Absolute Being, which is diffused through the phenomenal universe by a perpetual succession of emanations. Human personality is essentially unreal and would disappear if the veil of phenomena were removed. Jalálu'ddín Rúmí says in the Masnaví:

"There is no 'two,' unless you are a worshipper of form:
Before Him who is without form all becomes one.
When you regard form, you have two eyes;
Look on His light, which is single.
Necessarily the eye, when it falls on One,
Itself is one: 'two' is out of sight."

XXXIV

The Persian (W. 274) has "to demand from it the means of prolonging life" instead of "the Secret of my Life to learn."

XXXV

W. 32
"This jug was once a wretched lover like me,
Enamoured of the curls of beauty.
The handle which you see on its neck
Is a hand that once clasped the neck of a loved one."

XXXVI

The last line of the original quatrain (W. 252) is more explicit:

"I was a man like yourself: deal with me kindly."

Cf. 'Attár's apologue (*Mantiqu 't-Tair*, vv. 2345-2359) translated by FitzGerald and published in his *Letters and Literary Remains* (1890), vol. ii. p. 467.

XXXVIII

The last two lines were suggested by W. 136:

"This caravan of Life is passing on with wondrous haste:
Seize the moment that is passing merrily!"

XXXIX

Súfís use the phrase "This and That" (*ín u án*) to signify the multiplicity of phenomena contrasted with the Unity of God.

OMAR KHAYYÁM

XL

W. 196:
> "First, I will thrice divorce Reason and Religion,
> Then I will take the daughter of the Vine to wife."

"The daughter of the Vine" (*dukhtari raz*) is a hackneyed metaphor for wine, which is also styled 'the mother of iniquities' (*ummu 'l-khabáith*).

XLI

W. 336
> "I know the outward form of Not-being and Being,
> And I know the inward essence of everything, high and low alike.
> Nevertheless, may I be ashamed of my knowledge
> If I know any degree more exalted than drunkenness!"

This is perhaps a parody of the Súfí doctrine that the highest knowledge is gained through illumination and ecstasy.

XLII

FitzGerald has turned the "old man" of the original quatrain (W. 284) into "an Angel Shape."

XLIII

It is said in a Tradition of the Prophet: "My people shall be divided into seventy-three sects, and all of them shall be in the Fire save one sect." On being asked which sect would be that one, he replied: " That which I follow and my companions."

XLIV

Sultan Mahmúd of Ghazna (see note on stanza x.) is called "the victorious Lord" in allusion to his successful campaigns, as the champion of Islam, against "the misbelieving and black Horde" of Hindoo idolaters, who vainly offered him an enormous sum of money on condition that he should spare the famous idol of Súmnát. Cf. 'Attár's *Mantiqu 't-Tair*, v. 3100 and foll.

XLVI

W. 310:
> "This wheel of heaven, at which we stand amazed,
> We deem like unto a magic lantern:
> The sun is the lamp, the world is the shade,
> And we ourselves are the figures revolving on it."

The magic lantern of the East is sometimes a lamp with a revolving shade, on which figures are painted.

XLVII

W. 282:
> "Since at the last you will be nothing,
> Think that you are not, and, while you are, be merry!"

Notes

XLIX

W. 270:

> "We are all chess-men, and Heaven is the player
> In reality, not metaphorically.
> We play a brief game on the board of Life,
> And return, one by one, to the box of Non-existence."

L

This stanza (W. 401) alludes to the favourite Persian game of polo.

LI

W. 257:

> "Submit to Destiny and put up with affliction,
> For this Pen, having once written, will never go back for thy sake."

Moslems believe that the eternal decrees of Allah are inscribed by the Divine Pen on a tablet beneath His Throne.

LII

The comparison of the sky to a bowl turned upside down is common in Persian poetry.

LIII

This stanza appears to have been invented by FitzGerald, but many of the original quatrains express the same idea in different language.

LIV

W. 140:

> "On the day when they saddled the wild horse of heaven (the sun),
> And equipped Mushtarí and Parwín,
> This portion was assigned to me by the Registry of Fate.
> What sin have I done? This is my destined lot."

Mustarí is the planet Jupiter, and Parwín the Pleiades.

LV

'Súfí' is the Muhammadan term corresponding to 'mystic.' The word was originally derived from the garments of wool (Súf) which some early Moslems wore as a sign of asceticism. Here the Súfí stands as a type of sancitimonious piety. In later editions of the poem the Dervish, or religious mendicant, takes his place – an alteration probably suggested by the verb "howls" in the last line. There is a special order of 'Howling Dervishes' (the Rifáís), who utter loud barks and shrieks during the performance of their orgiastic exercises, but the practice is not confined to them.

LVI

"The one True Light" is God, whom the mystics of Islam generally call 'the Truth' (al-Haqq). They say that 'the Truth' is invested with attributes of Majesty (*Jalál*) – such as Wrath, Vengeance, etc., and attributes of Beauty (*Jamál*) – such as Love, Mercy, etc.; that the Majestic Attributes are reflected in the existence of Hell, the Beautiful Attributes in the existence of Paradise; and that Man is the Microcosm who reflects all the Attributes, beautiful as well as majestic, in himself. This is the explanation of W. 92:

> "Hell is a spark from our fruitless pain,
> Paradise a breath from our time of joy,"

and similar passages, which suggested to FitzGerald the magnificent stanza (lxvii. in his final edition):

> "Heav'n but the Vision of fulfill'd Desire,
> And Hell the Shadow from a Soul on fire,
> Cast on the Darkness into which Ourselves,
> So late emerged from, shall so soon expire."

The Persian original of the concluding distich is (W. 262):

> "If I tell Thee my heart's secret in the Tavern,
> That is better than to say my prayers without Thee in the Mosque."

The Tavern symbolises true adoration of God in the raptures of mystic love, while the Mosque (or Temple) indicates such formal and passionless worship as is rendered by the worldly.

LVII

In this stanza FitzGerald has kept closer than he usually does to the Persian (W. 432).

LVIII

This famous quatrain has no definite original, although parallels might be found for the greater part of it. But in the last words FitzGerald has out-Omared Omar. Cf. W. 265:

> "He made the (natural) law, which it is impossible not to obey,
> And then ordered us to refrain from following it.
> Thus every one in the world is helpless and desperate
> Between His command and His prohibition: *'tilt the jar but do not spill!'*"

LIX

Stanzas lix. to lxvi. make up the Kúza-náma, that is, the 'Pot-Book.' It was inspired by several Persian quatrains which represent God as a Potter moulding or breaking human crockery. The first two stanzas are little more than an amplification of W. 283:

> "Yestereve I went into a potter's workshop
> And saw two thousand pots speaking and listening.
> Suddenly one pot raised his voice and cried,
> 'He is the Potter and the pot-buyer and the pot-seller.'"

Notes

Ramazán, the ninth month of the Muhammadan year, is the Moslem Lent, during which nothing may be eaten between sunrise and sunset. The Muhammadan year being lunar, its months go the round of the seasons; and when Ramazán coincides with midsummer, the intense heat renders the Fast extremely fatiguing. It is proclaimed on the next day after the new moon has been seen, and is ended on the appearance of the new moon – here called "the better moon" – of Shawwál (the following month), which is anxiously looked for.

LX

According to the Súfí doctrine of 'Unification,' Potter and pot are essentially one (cf. note on stanza xxxii). Similarly Báyazíd of Bistám, a celebrated Persian pantheist, said:

"I am the wine-drinker and the wine and the cup-bearer."

LXII

W. 42:
"The cup which He moulded and put together –
How can He think right to break it in a fit of drunkenness?
All those lovely heads and feet and hands –
For love of what did He make them? For hate of what did He break them?"

LXIV

W. 193:
"They say that at the Resurrection harsh words will be spoken
And the Almighty Friend will be severe.
Only kindness can come from Absolute Good:
Be cheerful, for it will end well."

LXVI

W. 218:
"The month of Ramazán is past, and Shawwál has come,
The time of mirth and pleasure and song has come.
The hour has come when people cry, 'Shoulder the wine-skins!'
For the porters, jostling one another, have come."

"The little crescent" is "the better moon" of stanza lix. (*q.v.*), whose appearance marks the expiration of the Fast and the commencement of a feast lasting for three days.

LXVIII

W. 17:
"I will drink so much wine that the odour of the vintage
Will come forth from my dust when I go under the dust;
So that topers who visit my sepulchre
Will be made tipsy and dead-drunk by the fumes of my wine."